WORLD'S GREATEST ATHLETES

Shaun WHITE

By Jim Fitzpatrick

The Child's World
www.childsworld.com

Published in the United States of America by The Child's World®
1980 Lookout Drive • Mankato, MN 56003-1705
800-599-READ • www.childsworld.com

ACKNOWLEDGMENTS

The Child's World®: Mary Berendes, Publishing Director

Produced by Shoreline Publishing Group LLC
President / Editorial Director: James Buckley, Jr.
Designer: Tom Carling, carlingdesign.com

Photo Credits: Cover: Corbis.
Interior: AP/Wide World: 15; Corbis: 7, 10, 21; Getty Images: 1, 3, 5, 8, 16, 19, 22; Joe Robbins: 12; Mark J. Rebilas/Robbins Photography: 27, 28.

LIBRARY OF CONGRESS
CATALOGING-IN-PUBLICATION DATA

Fitzpatrick, Jim, 1948–
  Shaun White / by Jim Fitzpatrick.
    p. cm. — (The world's greatest athletes)
  Includes index.
  ISBN 978-1-59296-883-1 (library bound : alk. paper)
  1. White, Shaun, 1986- 2. Snowboarders—United States—Biography—Juvenile literature. I. Title. II. Series.

  GV857.S57F578 2008
  796.93092—dc22
  [B]

CONTENTS

The Flying Tomato Strikes Gold

IN EARLY 2006 MUCH OF THE SPORTING WORLD'S attention was focused on Torino (Turin), Italy, a small town in Europe's southern mountains. Snow-covered Torino was the site of the 2006 Winter Olympic Games. Perhaps they should have been called the "Shaun White Games," because Shaun emerged as the Winter Olympics' biggest star. Snowboarding's wonder-kid was greeted in the streets of Torino with chants of, "Il Pomodoro Volante!" Was that a new pizza? A type of pasta? No, it was Italian for White's nickname, thanks to his red hair: The Flying Tomato.

By the time of those Winter Games, Shaun was already a snowboarding legend. He was famous in that world for his ability to nail a winning run at the last possible moment.

At the Olympics, he did it again, falling in the first qualifying run before swooping into the finals on his last run. "Sometimes it comes down to just having to make it," explains White. Part of what separates White from the pack is his ability to perform in those pressure-filled moments.

In the finals, he came through again. When the scores were posted, he was the Olympic **halfpipe** champion! He went from just being known in the small world of snowboarding to being famous all over the world.

This amazing athlete wasn't finished, however. In 2007 he became the first athlete to win X Games gold medals in two different sports, snowboarding and skateboarding. His victory in 2007's vert skateboarding event came on his last run, with the pressure on again.

Golden Tomato! Shaun shows off his Olympic gold medal in 2006.

Read on to find out more about this marvelous multi-sport star.

Young Shaun had trouble finding gear that fit him. His mom found him a **sponsor** after they saw his video clips!

CHAPTER 1

In a Hurry to Reach the Top

SHAUN, WHO WAS BORN IN CARLSBAD, CALIFORNIA, in 1986, was only six when he tried snowboarding for the first time. Shaun almost didn't get the chance, however. When he was just an infant, he had to have surgery on his heart to correct a **birth defect**. The surgery worked, and Shaun grew up ready for action.

Shaun's parents, Roger and Kathy, were ready for it. Shaun's older siblings (brother, Jesse, and sister, Kari) loved snowboards and skateboards. They surfed at San Diego beaches near Carlsbad, and the family would drive to June or Mammoth Mountains in California's Sierra Nevada Mountains to snowboard.

Shaun's excitement for action was so dramatic that Kathy wanted to slow him down to keep him from hurting himself. At the time, equipment sized for young snowboarders was hard to find. This was a good thing from Kathy's point of view. It meant Shaun had to use oversized snowboards and boots, resulting in slower maneuvers. Kathy also slowed him down by making him ride with his right foot forward. This was backwards (called "switch stance") for Shaun because he's a natural "regular foot," or left foot forward.

Regardless of his mother's concerns, Shaun focused on learning to snowboard. His brother Jesse recalls, "He was jumping off little bumps right from the beginning, and he was making them, too!"

Within a few years Kathy realized there was no holding Shaun back. She contacted Burton Snowboards to find scaled-down equipment that would be safer for the eager Shaun to use. The Burton people were curious about Kathy's claims about Shaun's ability. Could a little kid really do everything she said he could do?

When she sent them a videotape of Shaun doing awesome snowboarding moves, they believed and became one of his sponsors. Shaun was given high-quality gear made just for his size. His snowboarding skills began to develop more quickly than ever.

The U.S. Open Snowboarding Championships were first held in 1982 in Vermont. It has become American snowboarding's top annual event.

By 2001, Shaun was soaring with the big boys. Here he competes in Utah in a snowboarding World Cup event.

The family added trips to Windell's Snowboard Camp at Mt. Hood in Oregon. Camp director Tim Windell recalls, "We almost didn't take Shaun, because he was only six or seven at the time, and we'd never had such a young camper. But he was an incredible athlete, even at that time."

Soon, Shaun was dominating **amateur** events. At 12, he entered his first **professional** competition, the U.S. Open. "In the amateur contests I had a run I felt I could always win with," recalls Shaun, "but once I turned pro I was pushed to learn new stuff."

Young Shaun White

Although "The Flying Tomato" may have seemed obvious because of his wild red hair, that's not the only nickname Shaun has earned. When he was younger, his nicknames included "The Egg" and "Future Boy." "The Egg" came from the fact that his white snowboarding helmet was a bit oversized. Remember, snowboarding is still a relatively new sport. When he started, he couldn't find child-sized gear. So when he flew down the slopes, his helmet-covered head looked like an oversized egg!

It wasn't too long, however, before "The Egg" became "Future Boy," because White's snowboarding abilities seemed to develop at such a quick pace. Everyone realized he was filled with **potential** . . . his future seemed unlimited on a snowboard.

No matter what name or nickname Shaun is called, you can call him one thing for sure: a winner.

The new "stuff" included bigger **airs** and an ability to put together tricks on his halfpipe runs one after the other. This was much like superstar Tony Hawk's ability on skateboard ramps. "I first met Shaun while snowboarding when he was about nine or ten," explains Hawk, skateboarding's living legend, "and then we started skateboarding together, too. Back then we spent a lot of time skating the ramps at the Encinitas YMCA." The result was that Shaun picked up another sponsor. Hawk's company, Birdhouse Skateboards, began giving Shaun his skateboarding equipment.

In 2002, Shaun had a setback that motivated him to do even better. He missed qualifying for the U.S. Olympic snowboarding team by 0.3 points!

The moves he perfected on the snow helped turn 10-year-old Shaun into a top skateboard artist as well.

Here's Shaun at the X Games, one of his greatest skateboarding sites, doing a "grab" during the **vert**.

Even without Shaun, the U.S. team won men's and women's golds in the halfpipe event at the Salt Lake City Olympics. But Shaun was more dedicated than ever to establish himself as a top pro snowboarder. He took a big step toward that goal the next year when he won gold medals at the Winter X Games for halfpipe and **slopestyle**, and at the U.S. Open in slopestyle.

As a skateboarder, he was rapidly improving, too. He entered his first pro skateboarding contest, the Slam City Jam in Vancouver, Canada. Later in 2003, he finished sixth in the Summer X Games skateboarding halfpipe. Was it possible for White to be so successful in both sports? Was he a snowboarding champion who was beginning to do well as a skateboarder, or was he a skateboarder who had done remarkably well as a snowboarder?

The answer is that he's pretty much a star in both. In addition to his 2006 Olympic gold medal, he's won 12 X Games snowboarding medals (8 gold, 3 silver, 1 bronze). He is the only athlete to participate in both the Winter and Summer X Games. In 2006 he won the ESPY Award (given out by sports cable channel ESPN) as the Best U.S. Olympian and Best Male Action Sports Athlete. In 2007, he captured two first places in the Dew Tour's skateboarding halfpipe competitions. The experience he gained in those events helped him become the first to win X Games gold medals in both snowboarding and skateboarding.

CHAPTER 2

From One Halfpipe to Another

SHAUN'S VERSATILITY IS ONE THING THAT SETS him apart from other great action sports stars. His first gold medal "cross-over" came when he won the halfpipe and slopestyle competitions in the 2003 Winter X Games. It was a big deal because no one else has accomplished the feat. The two styles of snowboarding call for very different types of skills. It is very difficult for one athlete to succeed at both.

Slopestyle presents a series of different obstacles to the snowboarder as he rides downhill. The rider performs different jumps or maneuvers at each embankment, quarter-pipe, handrail, or gap. Judges score these runs for the rider's ability and creativity. Being able to change a move based on the snow conditions is a big part of slopestyle success.

Shaun rides a rail during a 2006 slopestyle event. Obstacles like this are part of navigating a slopestyle course.

Halfpipes, meanwhile, are U-shaped gullies carved from snow, with vertical side walls sometimes reaching as high as 17-20 feet. The halfpipe's "transition"—the area where the slope changes—is where the flat bottom swoops to the vertical side. The size of the transitions, the height of the walls, and the slope of the halfpipe all affect the riders' choices of moves. A halfpipe gives the rider

Here's a good look down a halfpipe course. You can see the U-shape, the high sides, and the long, downhill run.

chances to create a run based upon its basic size and dimension. Slopestyle riders adjust to a series of different obstacles that are completely different from each other. While halfpipes are all basically the same shape, each slopestyle course is different.

Because of his success in both, White might be compared to a runner who can do well while sprinting around a track as well as while running through the woods in and around trees.

To this ability to perform different skills, Shaun adds one more item: skateboarding. Some might say, "Skateboarding's just like snowboarding, just without snow, right? What's the big deal?"

The big deal is that, although the sports are similar, there is one important difference— snowboards are attached to the rider's feet, while skateboards are not. Skateboarding tricks must be accomplished without falling off or losing the board. That can't happen in snowboarding. The smaller skateboards also let riders perform more difficult types of tricks. One thing is certain in looking at the two sports: on land or snow, Shaun White rules halfpipes!

CHAPTER 3

Shaun's Global Board Ride

SHAUN'S WINTER OLYMPIC GOLD MEDAL BROUGHT the world to his door. In fact, Shaun's global travels were the theme of a series of ads that show Shaun moving from continent to continent looking for better snowboarding conditions. In the ads, Shaun leaps from airport to airport looking for snow.

Tony Hawk, a world-traveler in skateboarding, says, "It's crazy right now for Shaun. He literally doesn't know where he is! He's just 'all over the place,' in every sense of the word! That whole [American Express ads] thing, where it shows him in South America, and the next day he's in Europe, and then the next in Asia or Montana—that's not so far from the truth. That's actually sort of what his days are really like!"

Superstar! One of the cool things about being an Olympic star is hanging with Hilary Duff at the 2006 Nickelodeon Awards.

As White explains, "I've been going nonstop since I was sixteen," when he first entered that professional skateboarding contest in Canada.

Words From the Master

Tony Hawk knows success like few other action sports athletes. He knows it isn't something that just happens. Success is the result of long hours and dedicated effort. "Shaun has been skating nonstop, almost every day, to reach this level," Hawk said about his friend's 2007 X Games gold medal in vert skateboarding. "He's even been calling me on the weekends so we could go skate the ramps together . . . he's just really been dedicated, and he's focused on learning new tricks. Not just big whirly things, either, we've been trying to teach him basic lip tricks that are more technical, and he's making them now."

In fact, Hawk believes it's the more technical tricks that have elevated White's success to the X Games gold medal. "The idea that he can pull a backside lipslide in between a '5' and a McTwist," explains Hawk, "shows everyone, including the judges, that he's a total skater. These new tricks he's learned have really lifted him to a new level."

It turns out the weekend skate sessions aren't just about skating the ramps for Hawk. "It's been great for me," he explains, "because I take the keys to Shaun's newest Lamborghini and take my kids for rides around the neighborhood. They really dig it!"

A boyhood friendship with skateboard legend Tony Hawk (right) gave Shaun someone to talk to about his new, wild life.

"I compete in the summer in skateboarding, and in the winter in snowboarding. That really helps me out because I get stoked on skating, and by the time I'm like, 'This is boring,' it's time to go snowboarding! I kept thinking that, after the Olympics, things would slow down a little bit, but, really, they haven't."

Shaun's Big Moment

Shaun has had a lot of amazing moments on the slopes and vert ramps of the world. But none was bigger than his gold-medal run at the 2006 Winter Olympics. It was a run, however, that he almost didn't make.

In Olympic snowboarding, all riders have to make qualifying runs. The top scores from these runs make it into the finals. During Shaun's first run, he fell once and

didn't do nearly as well as he—and everyone else—had expected. His score was so low—seventh place—that he was in danger of not making the final. His Olympic dream nearly ended at that point.

U.S. snowboard coach Bud Keene took his young athlete away from the crowds around the halfpipe. They went to a quiet area and just rode some easy trails to calm Shaun down. He knew he had a better run in him.

"Every time I've had a bad performance at an event," he later told *USA Today*, "I've come back more determined and focused to succeed."

Returning to the halfpipe for his second run, he put up a score that shot him up to second place.

In the finals, each snowboarder also got two runs. In his first run, Shaun put the gold medal out of reach. His score of 46.8 was just short of a perfect score of 50. He launched into the air six times during his gold-medal ride, spinning a total of 13 times around. His awesome aerial display (left) was good for gold.

In his second run, with the gold assured, he put on a show for the fans. He made them cheer with some lip-slide tricks that normally wouldn't thrill judges but that the Italian fans loved. "I just started to have some fun," he said afterward. Fun . . . with a golden touch.

With snowboarding's growth and acceptance White now finds a world that simply didn't exist when he was younger. U.S. dominance of Olympic snowboarding has helped convince many North American ski resort owners to embrace the sport. They are building more and more snowparks and halfpipes for snowboarders. More ski resorts are adding snowboarding as it loses its reputation as a

Snowboarding and sledding indoors? The growth of the sport led to the creation of this indoor snow palace in Dubai.

sport for wild riders. While fewer people are skiing these days, more and more are snowboarding. In fact, some "ski" resorts have left skiing behind and become all-snowboarding areas.

In fact, the world's largest indoor snowpark opened recently in Dubai, in the Middle East. With more than two dozen indoor snowparks throughout Europe, snowboarding is becoming an indoor option for many.

As his two sports continue to grow in popularity around the world, new opportunities for Shaun White seem limitless. For instance, his longtime friendship with Tony Hawk has helped him become involved with projects that give young people the same chances Shaun enjoyed. He's been a consistent supporter of the "Stand Up for Skateparks" program that helps the Tony Hawk Foundation build more places for kids to learn to skateboard.

Shaun also recently traveled to Rwanda in Africa, where he visited orphanages and gave away skateboards in an effort, he says, "To take their minds off things." Turns out that Shaun is all-world in helping out, too.

A study by Syracuse University showed that the number of people taking part in snowboarding more than doubled from 1995 to 2005.

CHAPTER 4

What Is "Future Boy's" Future?

WHERE DOES "FUTURE BOY" GO FROM HERE? BACK to the Olympics is one possibility. The 2010 Winter Games are set for Vancouver, British Columbia. But the Summer Olympics might also be in his future, too. Skateboarding might be added to the Summer Games in 2012 in London, England. Might Shaun win gold medals in both the Summer and Winter Olympic Games? "It's not outside my view!" he says.

For now, though, his plans include completing his new home in southern California, working on video productions for skateboarding and snowboarding, and helping to design video games based upon his abilities in both sports. Of course, he'll continue to travel the world seeking new experiences in snowboarding and skateboarding.

High Flying Tomato! Shaun gets big air on his way to a gold medal at the 2007 X Games, held in Los Angeles.

The business of sports—product **endorsements**, special appearances, and other demands for his time—is all part of the success Shaun has created for himself. Not bad for a guy who just celebrated his 21st birthday in 2007 and was already an Olympic champion and X Games champion.

"People are talking about skateboarding being part of the Olympics," says White, "For now, I'm just trying to skate as much as I can. Hawk is the best out there, and he's spent so much time skating with me, and I've learned so much from him. So, I'm still learning. I'm still trying to get better and learn new tricks. I've been skating with Tony at his ramp, and I hope I can just learn as much as I can."

Shaun flashes a winning smile after he lands safely during the 2007 X Games.

Which may be a troubling message for White's fellow competitors, in snowboarding and skateboarding—he's trying to learn more and get better. That sounds like a champion in any sport.

Shaun White's Career Achievements

SNOWBOARDING

► **WINTER OLYMPICS:** 2006 gold medal (halfpipe)

► **WINTER X GAMES:** 2003, 2006, 2007 gold medals (halfpipe)

► **WINTER X GAMES:** 2003, 2004, 2005, 2006 gold medals (slopestyle)

► **U.S. CHAMPIONSHIPS:** 2005, 2006, 2007 first place

► **WORLD HALFPIPE CHAMPIONSHIPS:** 2007 first place

More than 15 first-place finishes at individual halfpipe events around the world

SKATEBOARDING

► **SUMMER X GAMES:** 2007 gold medal (vert)

► **DEW TOUR EVENTS:** 2007 Cleveland–first place, 2007 Baltimore–first place, 2006 Denver–first place, 2005 Louisville–first place

GLOSSARY

airs   nickname for tricks performed in midair in snowboarding or skateboarding

amateur   a person who is not paid to do a job or take part in a sport

birth defect   a physical problem in a person that is discovered right after birth

endorsements   when an athlete or celebrity is paid to let his or her name be used to sell a product or promote a service

halfpipe   the U-shaped half-tunnel on which snowboarders ride

potential   the possibilities or promise of the future

professional   a person who is paid to do a job or play a sport

slopestyle   a way of snowboarding that involves going over and around obstacles

sponsor   when a company pays an athlete to wear its clothing or gear to help sell its products

vert   short for vertical, it means straight up and down; it's also a skateboarding event run on a wooden halfpipe

BOOKS

Skateboard Stars
By *K.C. Kelley*
(Child's World, 2008)
Shaun and Tony are not the only action stars around. This book features the top male and female skaters in the world.

Snowboarding
By *Clive Gifford*
(DK Publishing, 2006)
Want to follow in Shaun's board paths? This book gets you started in snowboarding, with details about gear, tricks, and safety.

Tony Hawk
By *Jim Fitzpatrick*
(Child's World, 2007)
Read about the man who is Shaun's buddy—and a world-famous skateboarding star!

WEB SITES

Visit our Web page for lots of links about Shaun White: www.childsworld.com/links

Note to Parents, Teachers, and Librarians: We routinely check our Web links to make sure they're safe, active sites—so encourage your readers to check them out!

INDEX

ABOUT THE AUTHOR

Jim Fitzpatrick has been an active skateboarder since 1957. He grew up to become the editor of Transworld's *Skateboarding Business* magazine. "Fitz" is currently vice-president of USA Skateboarding. He still skateboards every day, and lives in Santa Barbara, California, where he goes to Santa Barbara Montessori School (he's the principal!) with his three grandsons.